A Short Report
on the Fire
at Woolworths

Selected New and Old Poems
1980 – 2010

Stephen E. Smith

Main Street Rag Publishing Company
Charlotte, North Carolina

Author photograph by David Young

ACKNOWLEDGMENTS

Grateful acknowledgement is made to the editors of the publications in whose pages these poems appeared: *Green River Review, Pembroke Magazine, Cairn, Poetry Northwest, International Poetry Review, American Literary Review, The Pilot, PineStraw, St. Andrews Review, Kudzu, Montana Review, Southern Poetry Review, The Cape Rock, Apalachee Quarterly, Muse, Poets On, The Arts Journal, Buffalo Spree, Loblolly, Passion for Industry, Interim,* and *Quarterly West.*

"Michael," "Most of What We Take Is Given," and "Coming Back to the Old Emptiness," appeared in the *Anthology of Magazine Verse and Yearbook of American Poetry,* 1985, 1986, 1989.

"Cricket Poem" and "Michael" appeared in *Light Years* 1985, 1987, Bits Press, Case Western Reserve University.

The epigraph on page 47 is from *no thanks* by e.e. cummings. Copyright 1935 by E.E. Cummings. Reprinted by permission.

The epigraph on page 100 is from The *Civil War in North Carolina* by John G. Barrett. Copyright 1963 by the University of North Carolina. Reprinted by permission.

Library of Congress Control Number: 2010933614

ISBN: 978-1-59948-257-6

Produced in the United States of America

Main Street Rag
PO Box 690100
Charlotte, NC 28227
www.MAINSTREETRAG.COM

to Shelby Stephenson, Danny Infantino, Larry Allen, and Craig Fuller
with gratitude for the harmonies

Contents

II

Stephen E. Smith

I

A Short Report on the Fire at Woolworths

Remember this: a man is just as likely to giggle when he meets his executioner as he is to melt. The exquisite thing, the real and true talent, is to be able to raise tears to the throat, to the brims of the eyes, and then to convert those tears to laughter.

"The Wounded Soldier"

George Garrett

Most of What We Take Is Given

Believing the abandoned farm houses
and burned-out mobile homes held no meaning,
I spent my twenty-first year driving between
the Piedmont and the Carolina coast,
my foot to the floorboard between the tiny
crossroads whose names were Hayne, Stedman,
and Gumbranch, my eyes on the highway,
counting the yellow lines that ticked by like
seconds till I'd see the woman I believed was
waiting. These trips began in summer, heat devils
and tobacco blossoms shimmering, my mind
too manic to discern any singular detail,
but in the fall, a mile or so west of Beulaville
on a curve that dropped steeply down an escarpment,
I noticed a pony tethered to a fence post.
The pony was red, the color of the damp clay bank
against which it had, in all likelihood,
stood the previous summer, and I reasoned
that only the yellow poplar leaves drifting
the embankment served to silhouette the pony.
All that fall and early winter the pony
simplified my predicament: its suffering—
if indeed it was suffering—was not of its making,
and certainly it could will no circumstance.
It seemed unaware of the passing trucks
and cars, the weeks, the months, even the rain
that fell and turned its thick coat a dark brown.
And I began to believe that it all came down
to the casual drifting of leaves, a randomness
that must, finally, strip away all dignity.
Late winter brought ice storms, snow, mist
rising from the ditches and swamps, the Cape Fear
deep and filthy beneath the bridge I crossed

each Friday and Sunday. I recall an afternoon
in late February, the pony standing motionless,
wet snow clinging in heavy knots to its mane,
its eyes, as always, fixed on a patch of
gray earth. By then I knew it was ending.
I suspected, in fact, that the woman had taken
a new lover. I cannot now blame her, time and
distance being what they are, and it is best
to remember her standing in a doorway,
arms crossed below her breasts, her face
composed in silence, as if to ask a question.
It was April, and the highway west could
have been a green tunnel leading me anywhere.
I did not notice the red pony that afternoon,
and believe now that it had simply faded
into the sameness of the clay bank
against which it had stood waiting.

Stephen E. Smith

Whatever There Was To Say

A sky the pallor of hands folded in a casket.
You are driving south on Church Street this November
afternoon, and as you approach a railway crossing,
you notice a family, or what you believe
to be a family, walking the road—a man, a woman,
a boy, and a small girl, who is maybe eight.
The girl wears a blue print dress and is barefoot
in this late chill. And because the sky is the gray
of your grandmother's hands, you recall how that
old woman embraced you years ago as you sat in the
Avalon Theatre watching the movie news, the face
of a shivering child, a girl about the age of this
small girl, waiting beside a death camp railway.
Your grandmother put her arms around you in
the darkness and you were embarrassed, felt awkward:
an old woman clinging to you, a child of eight,
in a crowded theatre. But your grandmother is a long
time dead and you have come to understand that shoeless
children are, these days, simply shoeless children:
you've seen so many and so much worse.

Yet there is something about this family,
this child, her straight yellow hair cut
at such a ragged angle, the thin face, eyes set
deep in shadow. And her brother in a green cap,
her father, tight-waisted in blue trousers,
the mother in a heavy, white-flecked overcoat.
They carry plastic bags filled with aluminum cans
gathered from the roadsides and ditches. And haven't
you seen these very faces in photographs of Jews,
Gypsies, Poles, eyes blank with resignation, fatigue,
awaiting the gas chamber, clutching their belongings,
as if those few scraps of cloth could be of some value

where they were going? You wonder about this family,
wonder if the future of this small girl is as clear
as the past in photographs. Wonder how these church
steeples dare to rise straight into the smoky skies
of this most terrible of centuries. How neatly they
weave themselves among the bare branches of oak and
sycamore! And haven't you finally come to understand
that whatever there was to say cannot be said?
Which is probably what your grandmother was telling
you in the darkness of that long ago matinee
when she held you hard against her as you watched
that child shivering beside the death camp railway.
Remember how you tried to pull away and how she held
on tight, as if that simple, desperate gesture
might make a difference in such a world?

Stephen E. Smith

The Poet's Photograph

When I see a poet's photograph with the name
of the photographer printed below in tiny letters,
why do I believe the poet and the photographer
were once lovers? It's a ridiculous assumption.
Maybe the poet paid to have his photograph taken,
though I know this is seldom the case, or perhaps
the photographer was a faithful admirer of poets
and poetry, pleased to have been included in some
discreet yet significant way. And why when the poet's
wife snapped the shutter, do I believe they haven't
been lovers in decades?

And what of the photograph of the poet reading,
lean body bent over the lectern, his left hand
grasping air, his face drawn with intensity,
how do I know he went home with the photographer,
an attractive widow whose dead husband was
a kindly but obscure botanist who toppled one
spring morning into a variety of pinkish day lily
which bore his name, that after the cocktail party
she invited the poet to see her collection of rare
paraphernalia and that they tossed back a couple
of bourbons and tumbled straight away into the sack
where the poet recited Donne's "Love's Progresse"
and kissed gently her plump toes?

I'm sure it was raining that October night,
a warm panging on the tin roof, the lingering
scent of cinnamon air freshener, a blue neon light
flashing from the bar across the street, and that
in the morning they were both embarrassed, the poet
taking his leave somewhat awkwardly, and that he

never thought of the widow again until he opened a
letter forwarded to him in Greece where he was
languishing sans inspiration: *Came across this*
photograph—can it be so many years?—and thought
you might like it. I am married now to a botanist,
a kindly man who cannot make love because of recurrent
fibrillation. Will you be reading in this area soon?
And the poet studied the photograph of someone
who seemed a stranger and thought: the perfect
likeness for my next book.

Stephen E. Smith

Loose Talk

An article in this morning's *Observer,*
like other articles I've chance to read
on the life of Jane Mansfield,
notes that she was decapitated
when the car in which she was riding
crashed into a truck north of New Orleans.
This is what everyone who recalls
the buxom blonde remembers immediately —
like the neighbor who can tell you
that Walt Whitman was a homosexual
or that Catherine the Great
was a nymphomaniac who practiced bestiality.

The publicity photograph which
accompanies this article is not true to fact
or life: Mansfield is a brunette, smiling
a thick-lipped Monroe smile and thrusting
her breasts into the camera lens.
What would she have us believe — lover,
innocent, earthmother? In a faded tintype,
Whitman has gathered children about him.
He is affectionate, tender, ingenuous,
passionate, but certainly unaware of the
prurient obsessions which will one day
distort his finest lines. And who is
to say for sure that Catherine the Great
had a thousand lovers and left a poor
aroused pony dangling from the palace ceiling?

And what about the bewildered
man who came across a headless Jane Mansfield
on a highway north of New Orleans?
Did he recall the yellowing issue of *Playboy*

that lay creased beneath his mattress?
Could he see, if only for an instant, her nude
body arching, nipples erect, lips pursed?
Did he wonder: *Is this twitching flesh
the very same*? Did he ever find
the simple words to speak a simple truth?

Stephen E. Smith

Cleaning Pools

To my father

That summer you hired out to clean swimming pools
up and down Delmarva in your Willys truck,
the back end clanking with pumps and pipes,
cans of HTH, diatomaceous earth and alum,
and hauled me along to skim from the chlorined
waters hopeless, deluded toads and the clotted
bodies of insects.

I was ten that summer but can remember
how the surface of each pool was a surprise,
the water still clear or gone cloudy,
the blue bottoms flecked with algae
and the shimmering coins I retrieved for baloney
sandwiches and sodas at the Royal Oak Grocery.
You'd place a hand on my shoulder and say,
"Dive deep and get us that lunch money."

Do you recall the August afternoon at the Talbot
County Country Club, the thirty-six filter bags
we pulled and laundered, the steel rings so tight
our fingers bled? It was a five-hour job
and when the bags were back in place,
you dropped a pipe wrench clanging to the bottom.

It was five more hours in the high beams
and neither of us spoke till the filter
lid was clamped and screwed down tight.
Then we leaned against the truck and shared
a warm soda. Sheet lightning streaked
over the Chesapeake, and I began to notice
how after each flash, I went momentarily blind.
"It's strange," you said, finally, and without

my having spoken a word, "how quickly the pupil
closes to the light and how complete the darkness is.
It must be like dying."

Tonight I watch a storm gather over Carolina,
the lightning so intense the billowing undersides
of clouds are illumined from horizon to horizon,
each flash stealing me into shadow. Perhaps,
as you said, it is like death, this sudden light
and inevitable darkness. Or perhaps it is the
purest grace. It says what fathers and sons
mostly cannot say: It is the quick chill of a hand
on my shoulder, it's like plunging deep
into the pure, blue waters of the rich.

Stephen E. Smith

Love

"Don't ever use that word in a poem."
>   —advice from a friend

In my post office box this morning I find an article
in some pulpy TV tabloid detailing how
actor Franchot Tone was nearly beaten to death
in 1951 by ex-boxer-turned-actor Tom Neal:
a brain concussion, a broken nose,
the usual abrasions one must inflict or incur
while struggling over some sultry actress—
in this case Barbara Payton—
in some equally sultry Hollywood barroom.

And for a moment I'm there, leaning on the polished
bar—glasses of beer and gossip, Franchot and his
clever smile—when Tom Neal enters, flinging open
the door, sunlight swirling the cigarette smoke.
Violence was never gratuitous in the '50s:
the fist falls twice and the film fades
to the wedding, Franchot's face still bandaged
and Barbara Payton the blonde starlet smiling.

I smile, too, knowing that what we love
in lives of strangers is an inevitability
we perceive as just: Franchot bends Barbara back
onto the sofa bed, her blue eyes close, her mouth
opens. And the tabloid tells how Tom Neal died
in prison of congestive heart failure, Barbara
Payton a corpse at 39, too many pills,
how Franchot Tone succumbed to lung cancer in '68.

I tuck the tabloid under my arm and wander
into the April morning, dogwood blossoms drifting
the pink azaleas and children dancing on the grass,
their outsized radios blaring the old affliction.
A man holding a single red rose is arguing
with a women in a white sun dress. He turns away,
dropping the rose on the sidewalk, and her bare
shoulders go suddenly limp, as if to ask, of no one
in particular, a question too delicate for words.

Stephen E. Smith

Touring the Alamo in the Aftermath of the First Gulf War

As we circle San Antonio, the erudite Texan
seated beside me attempts to impress a smiling
flight attendant: "Right here in my pocket I got me
two tickets to Oscar Wilde's *Our Town*."
And riding from the airport a machismo cabdriver
jokes how a woman raped on a dark street
identified her assailant as a Texan: "He had
a big belt buckle, a little tiny pecker,
and he bragged the whole time."
Sweet Jesus, is there no end to the ignorance?

This November morning a cold rain rolls
over San Antonio—the Alamo, the River Walk,
the ruins of the '68 World's Fair—
and I read in *Texas Monthly* how
Davy Crockett wasn't born on a mountain top,
seldom wore a coonskin cap,
and surrendered to the Mexicans,
how he was brought before Santa Anna
and claimed he was simply a tourist
who'd wandered into the Alamo,
a victim of hype and manifest destiny.

Makes no difference that the walls of the old mission
are buried beneath abandoned buildings and asphalt,
that Davy, who had more than a little savvy,
probably hid beneath a mattress during the final assault.
No doubt he came to understand that mindlessness,
even in the service of bravado, is still mindlessness.
And maybe Santa Anna was like the cabdriver
whose dark eyes smile as he whistles
"The Yellow Rose of Texas."
He knows that if ole Davy stood in Alamo Plaza
this morning he couldn't tell San Antonio
from Philly, Topeka, or Bagdad,
stumbling the street where Woolworths and Pizza Hut
have risen from the rubble of adobe walls.

Here's how I'd have it: let Davy Crockett
awaken in front of the Pay-Less Liquor Store,
have him hold Old Betsy (which, by the way, he left
for safe keeping in Tennessee) high as the Texas sky,
let him doff his corny coonskin cap and holler,
without a trace of cynicism:
"Be sure you're right, then lie about it!
God bless you Walt Disney!
Welcome to San Antonio, Oscar Wilde!"

Coming Back To the Old Emptiness

So my grandfather rises
from the depths of the Depression
to flail my father (then a child
younger than my small son)
with an electric cord
in the basement of the house
on College Avenue,
the scars visible fifty years later
on my father's back and thighs,
and etched deeper in all of us—
my brother, sister, and mother—
than that night's rage
meant to inflict.

My grandfather is dying tonight,
the madness of eighty years—
the drunken women he dragged home,
the gamblers and bootleggers for whom
his family gave up their beds,
the endless, unrememberable
moments of cruelty
told now with a sigh and the
closing of my father's eyes—
all of it crumbling,
like the demolition of an old hotel
collapsing room by room,
coming down absolutely
but in a motion all too slow.

I could see it otherwise,
from a distance and with dispassion,
but for the night my grandfather,

a born-again Christian and ex-drunkard,
opened a drawer filled with knives,
guns, clubs, ice picks, straight razors—
a collection of murder weapons
purchased from a local magistrate—
and told me the story of each,
laughing at the moment of death,
then held a silver dagger lightly
to my throat, grains of sweat
beading in his palm.

Because we suffer impossible love,
my father grieves tonight for his father
just as I grieve for mine,
and my son, safe in his bed,
will learn of these cruelties
only in a poem, which itself must
someday crumble, its dust rising in
final dissolution.

Stephen E. Smith

Dear Michael

Received your letter today
and though we must live with what we've become
I was reminded of that July afternoon
Mother dropped us at the Cambridge Skating Rink
and said to me, "Stay with your brother;
he's only six."

I did, too,
though Cathy Baker, her new breasts blooming
beneath a blue cashmere sweater,
skimmed a seductive orbit
just beyond my longing.
Stayed with you during the ALL SKATE
and the COUPLES ONLY and the twelve trips
to the snack bar for lemonade
and then to the men's room where we stood
balancing before the porcelain,
suffocating slowly in the sour drift
of urinal cakes.

I was there, Michael, maybe imagining
Cathy Baker hunkered on wheels, one foot extended,
or pirouetting center floor, floating
languidly backward, her girl's body half
out of control—when what must happen to everyone
who ceases motion happened to you: the world
rolled out from under. And to save your life
you put both hands in the urinal.

I had not yet learned the body is a vessel
we are passing through, and as you looked up at me,
your eyes groping for salvation, your pink

fingers frozen among the soggy cigarettes
and dead gum, I thought you were ruined forever.

Perhaps, as you said in your letter, this life
of averages spares no one, but I remember how
even at six you were you, and how solemn you seemed
when you asked me, "Want some spearmint?
How about a Lucky Strike?"

Cricket Poem

Swerving right at the corner of
Bay Ridge and Tyler
I grabbed a crippled five-legger
as he stumbled the Dodge floorboard.
The other ninety-nine crickets,
purchased for fish bait at Barlow's,
spilled from their coffin
into Saturday sunlight
and scurried off beneath
dash padding and seat backs.
I sat with the car door open,
that five-legged jiminy tapping
encyclopedia into my palm,
and wondered what ninety-nine
crickets could do to a Dodge.

Nancy Simmons and I went
down that night with the *Thresher*
deep into the sea-green backseat
of that fifty-three Dodge.
Off Chinquapin Round Road
the news died whining on the car radio
and I pleaded like a doomed sailor.
She was about to moan yes
when a cricket whispered in her ear
and another called from
the glove compartment.

Suddenly her sisters were singing
in sun visors,
her mother cajoling from beneath
the clutch plate,
her father screaming in the dome light,

cousins chittering in the heater vents,
neighbors gossiping behind
the dashboard,
the cricket tabernacle choir singing
in ninety-nine part harmony
Nancy Nancy Nancy Nancy
save yourself forever.

Stephen E. Smith

Bomb Dream

So you grew up in the 50s, did you?
And when you were maybe 12 or 13
you dreamed the bomb dream every night.
You remember the ole bomb dream, don't you?
The sticky ferment of puberty, vapor trails, breasts,
h-bombs and Eisenhower, how in this dream you'd waken
to the whine of air raid sirens,
how you climb out your bedroom window,
down the rose trellis, how you smile to see yourself
running through Poplar Woods, round Paper Mill Pond,
hustling your young self over to Cathy Baker's house.
I know you remember Cathy Baker.
She was the sweetest thing in your 7th grade class
and though you'd never spoken to her,
you did touch her hand once in a duck-and-cover drill,
her flesh light, deathless.
So you climbed in Cathy Baker's bedroom window
and there she was. Wasn't it wonderful how in the bomb
dream she waited, saved herself just for you?
And you and Cathy tumbled into her bed and made mad
passionate love until the bomb came and you were both
vaporized in the firestorm.
So what happened to the bomb dream?
Well, you turned 20, 25, 45, the air raid sirens never sounded,
Cathy Baker married an insurance salesman and moved
to Topeka, the dream died and you forgot all about it and her
until you happened into a room darker than dreams,
a nightmare with some Cathy Baker gone wrong.
Remember how after the passionless lovemaking
You'd roll over and dream the bomb dream again
but backwards?
Too bad there's not a snippet of the kid you once were
left in your grownup self, and it's a shame the bedroom

window is locked tight, maybe nailed shut.
And isn't it just awful how Poplar Woods is now
a Walmart parking lot, and Paper Mill Pond is a condo city
gone berserk? Well, not to worry, friend.
This poem isn't about you, and it sure as hell isn't about me.
And anyway it was just a dream.

Journal Entry

wallace pardons last Scottsboro
boy
the headline blares

patience
I tell my son as he fiercely
curves his crayon within the lines
of his coloring book
is what you must have

beyond my window the last of blue
light bends through the branches
of a dying oak & spreads a
tangled shadow across the oak floor
to where my son curls upon the rug

the wind weaves the shadow of dying
oak on dead oak

the headline blares
babe ruth's widow dead at 72

Hassam's *Washington Arch in Spring*
ca. 1890

Pausing at the edge of twilight
each figure in this painting wears
a hat. Knit of patient harmony
the rose light decants through the
viewer's eye and urges from the city
earth daffodils, tulips and a distant
Henry James.

A staid lady is foremost on this
avenue, gloved hands demurely caress
her gray gossamer gown. Pinoaks
etch the evening sky with dappled
orange and olive. At the curb a
two-steed landau waits to debark
a smiling robber baron. In the gutter,
a tubercular immigrant street sweeper
stoops to shovel up the horse shit.

Stephen E. Smith

Working for Dorsey

All that gray-blue summer
the pungency of fresh paint
lingered like guilt.
"Cut in those moldings faster
and don't leave no holidays,"
Dorsey mumbled between clinched teeth,
his rum crook bobbing ash.

Rainy Saturdays we poured
Mary Carter Roll-Hide into
empty Sherwin-Williams cans
so Dorsey could jack up materials,
and as the sun lulled
over the Chesapeake
at a dollar ten an hour
I slapped on one coat of
egg-shell white and heard
Dorsey swear it was two:
"Lady, that paint job'll last ya
ten years, maybe more."

Those nights I dreamed of cheap
paint blistering in the August sun,
of needling autumn rain seeping
insidiously between buckled siding,
the damp bay wind chilling
the bones of children.

The summer I was seventeen
I painted houses for Dorsey,
then flew away from the peeling
sashes and twelve-hour days.

I remember how the aluminum
wing vibrated against a sky
gone as gray as ash, and how,
as the plane described an
oblique ear-fiddling arc,
I looked down and saw those
pool-specked subdivisions
spread like lace
upon the Maryland countryside.

Scar

From the high branches of mimosa
I look down and see BT Barnhart,
his arm already cocked,
the gray pointed road rock
held lightly in his hand.
His arm snaps
and the rock floats up,
tumbling into memory.

There seems time enough to move,
time to slide easily aside,
to hear the rock rattle among
the branches, the pink blossoms
exploding in the August dusk.

But I do not move
and these forty years later
cannot explain why.
Each morning's mirror
asks that question
of the small triangular scar
below my left eye
which like regret
grows darker with age.

The Bureaucrat Ties His Shoe

He hears loose laces crackling on the concrete,
poses like the letter R, his mind reviewing in
triplicate some adolescent disenchantment with
footwear.

Kneeling to renew the bow, he sees the sun-raked
sidewalk from a child slant, recalls that child
hood was a nightmare of things in his shoe:
fiendish pebbles, bumbling insects, sock-snared
cockleburs, turned-under tongues, nail nibs
sprouting in a heel print.

The sun is warm on his neck, his pulse too quick
to savor the resurrection of a child's bemusement
with time. He stands stiff in his starched
collar, wonders how his life became a knot not
even Houdini could dissolve.

Nothing

We are driving east on Glebe Road
when a rabbit is caught
in the sudden snare of headlights.
My father eases off the gas,
downshifts, and the rabbit escapes
into marsh grass.
I'm twelve years old
and can think of nothing
but Nancy Simmons naked,
how at Paper-Mill Pond
I'd heard her laughter
and seen her pale body hidden
among the bleached reeds.
My father asks what I am thinking
and I cannot tell him
of breasts ripening
somewhere in this soft darkness.

Twenty-five years
and I'm driving with my son
on a summer night.
In the radio's blue glow
I see on his face
the look I could not see on my own:
the eyes of a startled animal,
life bearing down
with the instancy of light.
"What are you thinking?" I ask,
and he answers as we all must,
"Nothing."

Fluid Drive

Beneath my eyelids the instinct arched.
Nancy, we made air dances of the rung-dry
night, a frenzied jungle-limbed fandango
in the front seat of my fluid-drive Dodge.

Undreaming beneath me you were the old
felt self made suddenly sure. You hummed
"A Rose and a Baby Ruth" and I swooned
in the radio's blue light, my foot braced
against the deluxe heater.

In that perilous moment I rode that kite-
strung cradle, blood and bone wedged into
the wind, while Jurassic semi-s groaned
south on John Hanson Highway.

You made me feel so damn good I cranked
up that flat-head six and let it blast
to screaming blue blazes, emptied out
my pure self into one brightly astonished
night

shuddering on firewheels, fluid drive and
a dollar gas.

Stephen E. Smith

Fallout Shelter, October, 1962

The salesman's hands flutter like bird wings
as he describes the lead-lined chamber beneath
our feet, the "natural air filtration system,"
the human capacity (4), and our certain survival.
Then we make true descent: mother and sister first,
father and I to follow in the order in which
nuclear etiquette dictates, into an opaque gloom
where we study the pipe bunks, the portable toilet,
the shelves of canned goods: pears, sardines,
apricots.

Blue light warms from the shortwave (an option)
and our shadows gradually ascend the wall and ceiling.
"The four of you could survive down here
for two months, maybe more," he says,
and we look into each other's eyes, hearing
the sirens and the scuffle of neighbors
against the bolted door.

"We have a time payment plan," the salesman says,
as we rise from the dead, ascending into true light.
The shelter's steel door claps shut behind us.
An October breeze tumbles leaves about our feet,
and we stare deep into a high blue heaven,
a damp otherworldly death clinging like hope.

Delmarva

Child of wind and dark water
I'd wander out under the clear dome
of stars and ask myself *Where am I?*
How is it I came to be here?
And when the inevitable chill
of isolation gripped me,
I'd recall the night my grandfather
walked in waist-deep snow
from Trappe Station to Oxford
and how a country he knew
in the his very bones vanished—
roads, trees, houses, fields—
all of it buried beneath a drifting landscape.
I'd look up into the that random scattering of light
and tell myself: *I am here.*

Which is what my grandfather screamed
into a bitter wind knifing off the Chesapeake,
the path he'd struggled gradually effacing itself
and the night gone dead to language.
He'd tell me how,
without even the stars to guide him,
he knew precisely where he was,
knew every field and tree,
knew the houses and the roads
that lay beneath the drifts.
He could never explain how or why
he was blessed with such knowledge:
Wasn't anything I thought, he'd say,
it was something I just felt.

Stephen E. Smith

Something I just felt, I'd say the words
over and over as skeins of discordant geese
drifted down upon the Tred Avon
and a small wind rattled the marsh grass.
I'd scuff the peninsula
still firm beneath my feet,
and stare into the winter sky,
the cold stars etched above me,
impassive but persistent.

Advice

A full moon rose
through the chain-link fence
as my father lifted me over.
The Country Club pool
had been closed since dark,
but there we stood
staring into the pure
star-glazed water of the rich.
"We're as good as they are,"
my father whispered.

He plunged in naked.
I climbed the steel ladder
to the top of the high dive,
crawled to the board's
sandpaper edge and looked down.
What I saw was the bright
moon-struck face of a poor man
who'd had it up to here.
"Jump!" he yelled.

I told the truth: "I'm scared!"
"Listen," he called back,
"you'll never get anywhere
in this life unless you take
a chance once in a while!"
It was the only advice
the old man had ever given me:
I flung myself feet first
into the dark.

Stephen E. Smith

Believers, it was like no leap
a poet ever leapt.
I did not hang suspended —
even for a moment —
in the blue drift of air.
I did not see before me
the confused unfolding
of my life,
nor could I hear the voice
of Danny Chapman daring me,
ten years later,
to take the Newcomb Turnoff
at ninety.

I did not feel the splintered bones,
the broken promises,
the blackened eyes, the lost love.
And I sure as hell never
saw the fist
that would one night
extract three of my teeth
in the alley behind Sam Loray's
Tavern.

No, I dropped straight down
and sank into black water,
belched air at dead bottom,
then clawed my way back
to the night's thin surface.
I looked up into the Milky Way
and saw the bare stars
fewer than my mistakes.

"Help me! Help me!" I screamed.
And from the dark I heard
my father's voice.
"Boy," he said, "you jumped in,
you get yourself out."

Stephen E. Smith

The 1950s

To know how it was in the fifties
go to the nearest pay phone,
deposit a dime
and call home when you know
no one is there.

While the phone is ringing,
shut your eyes and imagine
at the other end of the line
daffodils and sunlight
(it's always a spring morning
in the fifties).

Recall whatever pleases you:
pineapple upside down cake,
Rosemary Clooney, Glass Wax,
a blue checkered tablecloth,
Almond Roca, HaloLights,
Gunther Beer, I Like Ike
buttons, Pablum, Ann Blyth,
tangerines—

but you must allow the phone
to ring for ten years.
When no one answers,
you'll know you've dialed
the right number.

A Three-D Afternoon in Easton, Maryland, Circa Sept. 1956

Danny Chapman's big brother George
tears my matinee ticket, hands me
the stub and the folded three-D glasses
and I descend the velvet-roped aisle
into the Avalon Theatre, gray sunlight
from beyond the padded double doors
fading like last week's coming
attractions.

Stampeding buffalo tumble into the
orchestra pit. Tommy Hash, a year
older than I and in Mrs. Gretzsinger's
fourth grade class, lifts his glasses
up and down. "Jeeze, neat!" he
whispers. We applaud for the credits.
George holds the EXIT door open and
I'm in the street,

the three-D glasses still on my face.
The sky is a reddish quilt of clouds and
Garrison's Hobby Shop is blurring out
of business just beyond my father's
red two-tone Chevy idling at the curb.

I have caught my ole man red-faced,
his hand on the gearshift knob.
"How's the world look through those
glasses?" he asks, dropping it into
first. "Jeeze, neat!" I answer, as
we run the red light at the corner
of Dover and Harrison.

Stephen E. Smith

Christmas Poem

I cannot write a Christmas
poem for you,
not with all those slick verses
oozing through the mail,
the schmaltzy music whining
on the radio.

But what I can do
is tell you of a December
afternoon in 1957
when I sat in Miss Cohee's
fourth grade class
listening to the radiators clank
and staring at my scarred desktop
and how Eddie Morgan,
hunched in the seat beside me,
looked up suddenly and whispered,
"It's snowing!"

I looked up too,
along with the rest of the class,
out the tall warped windows,
across the empty playground,
to Idlewild Avenue,
and saw that it was true:
the first gray-white dust just drifting
the blue cedars.

If you are an old believer,
even on this bluest of December days,
I would give you that pale afternoon,
the chalkdust scuffle of shoes
on the worn floor,
those children's faces
eager as light.

Short Note on a Cat Sleeping

a sleeping cat hears every sound
you once told me

today the November wind rattles
the window glass
& I watch a cat sleeping
gray paws upturned
a leg buried beneath his thorax
like a knot of silk
his tufted ears waiting

I toss an empty beer can into
the waste basket
& not a whisker twitches

how nice
after all this time
to think of you & how you lied
to me about everything
including cats

Stephen E. Smith

Walking the Moon

you didn't show up for the funeral
but I was there & saw your frail
corpse smiling
& you did just fine

after the stupid words & wasted
flowers I took time to recall that
july afternoon we sat in your parlor
& watched men walking the moon
someday I'd sure like to do that
you said

but like everyone you took what was
given & loved what you could
other men went to the moon
you walked one back alley block to
work & tapped out an amazing history
on your telegraph key
your red hair went white
your eyes grew more liquid
you dozed so often
& died

all things lost go to the moon
you once told us
& now the family believes
you're happy in some slow motion
heaven dancing about in all that dusty
desolation

there is just a skim of moon tonight
grandfather & I think of you
rest easy old man

it's enough you lived
your life so well so long
did not die by inches
somehow made this world your home

Stephen E. Smith

Sign for My Doctor's Waiting Room

The prognosis is terminal, yet you
have gathered here in this Naugahyde
limbo to hedge your bets, cut off
catastrophe at the pass. We ask
only that you observe these few simple
courtesies.

Those of you still sufficiently
alive should feign indifference,
play well your Pollyanna bravura of
nonchalance. The senile should mumble,
wring their palsied hands, hold the
glistening enticement of better time
in their limpid eyes. The rest of you
should wheeze, exercise your croaking
coughs, writhe in silent agony, etc.

Hopeless expectations may seem to taunt
you from the crisp pages of our plastic-
bound *Geographics*, but look as if you're
pensive, seek solutions within yourself,
recall old wives' tales, repeat mother's
good advice. Above all, you should smile:
do not look as if you're waiting here
for rigor mortis.

And no smoking.

A Short Report on the Fire at Woolworths

The night Woolworths burned
the doll babies in the toy department
were heard to call from the fire
for their mamas and the plastic
soldiers melted and oozed like sap
back into the parched wood.
In the pet department the fish boiled
in their delicate suspension, consumed
by that which sustained. The canaries
thrashed against the cage bars until
they dropped like cinders and were
released at last to the air.
Only the turtles survived, sucked in
their striped heads and waited out the
holocaust in puddles of ashy slime.
From the steaming aftermath they
staggered by the hundreds into the
tangled street where they were promptly
slaughtered by laughing children and
the wheels of departing fire trucks.

Stephen E. Smith

II

The Complete Bushnell Hamp Poems

The boys I mean are not refined
They cannot chat of that and this
They do not give a fart for art

No Thanks
ee cummings

I am famous for the beer
which flows from my hair.

Pete Winslow

Carolina Drought

Ten miles south of Raeford,
the earth brittle as a bone,
the sky rolls black over
swaying tobacco blossoms
and sand devils dance among
the rusting truck bodies
and burned-out mobile homes.

At the Pow-Wow Tent Revival
for Christ the faithful lift
up their hearts and pray for
rain. They put up their hands
and love Jesus. "Worship him,
worship him," they chant,
swaying like tobacco blossoms.

On highway 401 at the warm
fingers massage parlor the
whores cackle from the windows.
They crack their gum, they smile.
They know the meaning of
drought.

Spring at Red's Carolina Citgo

mostly us boys at red's citgo
pour peanuts in our pepsi
& fart
chew marsh wheeling cigars
bruise biceps
& spew lie after lie
just for the noise

but when marylou's horn honks
& she elbows her hot ass
against that chevy's blue fender
her yellow hair gone all which
ways in the april wind
we gotta cackle & hoot

red flashes us the finger
from behind the high-test pump
& we jostle against the window
hands like weasels in our pockets
just knowing he's out there
talking some shit to loose Marylou

back inside he don't smile
slides that toothpick east to west
cheeks tight as hitler's fists
a man like red can afford to be
mighty proud

but he gets to it soon enough
& says
tonight whilst you boys is watching
the hogs screw
I guarandamnteeya
I'll be milking the lizard
in ole marylou

Stephen E. Smith

Red's Letter

Marylou honey,

I'm writing this to say
that I guess maybe you're right
I shouldn't ought to just jump
out of bed afterwards &
pull on my britches.
I don't know why I do that
but I sure wish you hadn't told
Linda Kay Pusey cause I know
you did.

She came down to the Citgo with
her hair all twisted up in them
pink rubber things & bought
herself a Nehi & went on in
front of the boys about how I
wasn't the huggy-wuggy type.
I'm going to kill her.

Anyhow I don't know why I do
that but I can't change & so
I guess maybe we better not see
each other anymore
until next time.
Red

Slow Leak

wrenchhanded
red pauses hunkered on
the asphalt & says
a tire with a slow leak is
like cheating on your wife
ain't nothing you can do about
it but you know it's getting
out

he spits
drops a lug in a sunshattered
hubcap
you're hoping I won't find no
leak cause you know maybe I
can't fix it anyway

so what do I do? I ask

do like everybody else does
he says
just drop it in gear
put your foot to the floor
& wait for the whole fucking
world to go crazy

Stephen E. Smith

A Sinner Struck by Lightning

Course we'd heard of such a thing.
The preachers was always promising
& sure, pool-hall loafers do lots
of crowing, specially Saturday nights
when they've drunk themselves stupid
& lied themselves blue. Always
some hardass who must lift a fist
& scream, "Well, by God if it's a
lie let me be struck down! Let
the Lord Hisself strike me dead!"

But ole Spivey Baggett was pure proof.
That night years back Bushnell Hamp
& me was just boys getting home
best we could from a Baptist meeting
& we was toting them black slickidy
covered Bibles that weighed like
lead & we'd cut short Chinquapin
Round Road for Baggett's July-high
corn field, thinking we'd beat out
some thunder rolling up over Raeford
& praying Spivey Baggett wouldn't
hear us cracking them green stalks.

Everybody said Spivey was bred mean
& might just gut you for the fun of it.
Said his grandpappy rode with Bedford
Forrest at Fort Pillow & my mama swore
the Baggetts had been sleeping with their
sisters ever since so as to keep
the line evil & now they all had slopy
chins & flounder eyes on the sides
of their heads so they could see in

circles like all true-bred sinners
must. Everybody knew Spivey kept three
women (one a drunk Tuscarora & I ain't
sure about the rest) & that's not counting
his stoop-shouldered wife who spent
her life doffing bobbins night shift
at Kenny's & I recall once he thrashed
his three brats with an electric cord
& Doc Badder allowed how he'd seen
nothing as terrible, them babies
feverish & whimpering & when Doc went
for bandages they snuck into his
kitchen & ate all the giblets out of
some gravy he'd left simmering on the eye.

So there we was—Bushnell & me—duck-
walking the corn rows & believing we'd
about made it when one of them black &
tan hounds that can smell a quail egg
in the next county went to howling &
then came that voice whining like a tight
bow cross cold fiddle strings, "I'll
call the sheriff the damn sheriff the sheriff
do you hear? the damn sheriff the sheriff!"
& Bush & me peeked through them stalks
& seen him, Spivey Baggett, clogging
his porch, waving a shotgun, his spindly
arms scribbling the air & I figure how
he saw our faces between the ears &
changed his mind about the damn sheriff
cause he dropped to one knee & took
aim with that doublebarrel. Hell, I
could almost taste the birdshot.

Stephen E. Smith

& then sweet Jesus I swear it just
happened like in a lie you'd make up
or something. First my hair stood on
end & then I screamed & didn't know it,
like maybe somebody put a meat cleaver
through my skull & Bush & me just stood
there wide-eyed & stupid as a crease of
yeller lightning stepped down the sky &
heaved Spivey Baggett off his porch &
jackknifed him into the mudsills where
he lay like a pile of wet laundry,
steaming.

Course we'd just come from the Baptist
meeting & we had the preacher's word
for what happens to sinners & that
Bushnell Hamp, who was sure enough on
a short trip to hell, got religion
before Spivey had hit the ground & he
held up that never-opened Bible like
he was Moses receiving the commandments
& squealed, "Lord thou has smited the
sinner! Strike not these thy poor
servants!" or some such shit & his
grimy thumbnails was gouging that
black leather cover. Hell, he meant it!

Then we took off stumbling, scrambling,
mowing furrows through green corn & safe
at home we cooled our heels for a day or
two wondering if maybe hogs had eat the
corpse. Soon enough we heard the word
that Spivey was alive. Alive damnit!

Story went his wife & brats dragged his
carcass into their shack & sent for Doc
Badder & it was touch & go there for a
while. Just damn desperate his wife
(she was a bad-times Baptist turned
Catholic out of pure pain) called in a
priest to save Spivey's soul. Seems
they asked him to confess his sins &
he just spit & said, "Confess hell!
I'll tell you what I done cause I'm
real proud of it," & he did too. For the
next six hours. Then that priest
crossed hisself & mumbled some malarkey
& pronounced that Spivey Baggett was
most likely the devil himself.

Local preachers picked up on the story
& went to sermonizing on such subjects
as "The Sinner & his Just Desserts" or
"The Lord Strikes Down the Transgressor"
& they used made-up names so'd everybody'd
know it was ole Spivey & most folks
believed it was going to make a difference.
Course it didn't. Spivey climbed out of
bed a few days later & stumbled straight
to a whorehouse where he stayed drunk
for two weeks & after that he dropped
sinning part time & took it up as regular
work. During the war he got rich running
hooch & black-market meat & they say he
had an interest in that whorehouse at
Sugar Hill.

Last time I seen Spivey Baggett was when
I got back from Korea. He was hanging out
front of Norwood's Pool Hall going on about
how he'd dug up a fresh grave in Sampson
County & cut off the corpse's head with his
shovel & climbed a church steeple & left
it dangling from the cross for all the
Sunday school babies to see next morning.
Course all them loafers went to cackling
& called him a liar to his face &
questioned how come they'd heard nothing
about it & he said there was a considerable
amount they'd heard nothing about & they
all hooted & shook their heads & stared
at their brogans. Then Spivey he got
a look something like hate—or maybe
more like love—on his flounder face
& he lifted a fist to the sky & screamed,
"Well, if it's a damn lie may I be
struck dead! Do you hear?—if it ain't
the truth let God Hisself strike me
down!"

Now I can tell you there probably weren't
a true believer among that bunch. Let's
see, there was Leroy Pinrawes, Cooney
Stackhouse, Daughtry McLamb & Baskin Cole,
that crowd was always into something.
But them boys got serious real sudden
& stuffed their hands in their pockets
& took to clearing their throats & they
just sort of sidled off in one direction

or another. Fact is I kind of eased on
up the street myself.
Now I'll tell you what's the truth:
you don't need to be no damn Bible
thumper to understand that sooner or later
there comes a time when you just have to leave
a sinner alone with his God.

How the River Took Daughtry Mclamb

A cloud shadow came dark over the water
& Daughtry was gone

along with that paint-manged rowboat
he bought for fishing in the summer
of '54. I recall how he scraped & sanded
& caulked & finally in mid-river
went down in one minute. Baskin Cole
& I watched from the Peachbottom
Bridge as the current took him away, his
hands gripping the gunnels, his scared-
pale face blurring the sycamores
that shaded Crains Point.
Then that cloud shadow came over
the water & he was gone.
Quick as that.

They crated Daughtry up in a cedar box
& at the Peachbottom Baptist Church
we lowered him into that sweet-Jesus
earth. It wasn't two days later Hazel
came through & that river went into
the graveyard & took Daughtry again.
But this time we didn't find him.
No box or nothing. At Crains Point we
searched among the toppled sycamores
& found a few drowned cats, a hen house,
a bloated sow or two. But no Daughtry McLamb.

He'd gone off down the river
to wherever it goes.

Saturday, August 20, 1955

I ate me some brains and eggs for breakfast and about nine Fat Baskin Cole come over in his daddy's '51 Ford convertible and we spent three hours washing and waxing. We had dates for the drive-in with Lindsey Lou and Carol Lee and we figured our chances were better if the car looked sharp. I got Mama's new Electrolux and run me a wire from the kitchen window and vacuumed the carpet and scrubbed the mats. Mama and Daddy had gone to the A&P so Baskin and me swiped a six pack of Blue Ribbon out of the icebox and hid it in the trunk.

We put the top up on the Ford to keep the dust out and drove to the Toot & Tell It and got burgers and fries and milkshakes and watched girls drive through. Baskin said I ought to give him a $1.50 for gas and oil but I told him I'd be short for the drive-in so we siphoned some gas out of Daddy's John Deere. I told Baskin the inside of the Ford smelled like a mule fart so we took some of Daddy's Bay Rum and sprinkled it all over the seats and spent the rest of the afternoon riding around with the top down.

For supper I ate two pork chops, some pintos and three pieces of cornbread. Then I scrubbed under my arms and took a washcloth to my cod, just in case. I put on my best jeans and a black tee-shirt and rolled up a pack of Camels in my sleeve. I pulled on a fresh pair of white socks and buffed up my loafers. Baskin picked me up about eight and we swung by Carol Lee's and

Stephen E. Smith

then to Lindsey Lou's. Lindsey's mama said she had to be in the house by midnight and Lindsey said, "Yes Mama." But when she got in the car she called her mama "a pure T bitch."

The movie was stupid. The girls had hot britches for that James Dean guy, but I said the story didn't make no damn sense with him planting beans the way he did and making all that money. I kissed Lindsey Lou but she had bad breath so I walked to the refreshment stand and bought some doublemint which she chewed for about two minutes before she spit it out. It didn't help so I stuck my tongue in her ear and fiddled with the clasps on her bra but she wouldn't let me do nothing. I got the six pack of Blues out of the trunk and drank three hot ones real fast. I was pissed and I told Baskin to take us home, goddamnit. Lindsey Lou and Carol Lee wanted to watch the rest of the movie but I said, "Tough shit." At the front door Lindsey Lou wouldn't even hug me. "You know," she said, "sometimes you can be a real asshole."

Welcome to Sunrise Biscuits:
Found Poem

Please check your order
and count your change
before departing.

When you're gone,
we cannot be held
responsible.

Stephen E. Smith

Bushnell Hamp Chain-Drags a Blue Tick into Shorty's Tavern and Orders a Beer

"Is that cur-dog of yours a shit eater?"
BJ Baynard asks.

"I don't know," Bushnell says.
"Did he snap at you?"

How Fat Baskin Cole Eat
Hisself Out of a Wife

Carol Lee said to me, "Baskin Cole
you ain't nothing but a sway belly
hog. What I want is a man thin as
a sliver." And maybe I had been
rooting a little high on the trough,
all them biscuits and that lemon pie.

Course as it later developed
she'd been cooking up something
with BJ Baynard's boy Bobby all
along. That's where she is now,
living in his doublewide over near
Lobelia. Just breaks my heart
when that advertisement fella comes
on the TV and says, "I can put
you in this little honey now for
only $49.95 a month," and he points
at one of them mobile homes. Hell,
it just tears me all to pieces.

So I wrote Carol Lee this sweet
letter about how my hair was still
curly and my eyes still blue and
how if tears was them calories she
was always going on about, why there
wouldn't be enough left of ole Baskin
to get a regular hug on. But it
didn't do any good. That woman
will no longer listen to me.

So most every night now I'm down
here at Shorty's drinking this
special diet beer & tilting the
pinball machine. Sometimes I punch
"Your Cheating Heart" into the jukebox
& it seems like Hank is singing
that song just for me.

Bushnell, I can tell you what's the
truth, ain't nobody in this whole
damn world feels sorry for fat.

Bushnell Hamp Tells About the Friday Night Fight Down at Shorty's Tavern

Somebody has slaughtered a hog!
I thought first
but it was just Lacy Brockmoor's
steel guitar squealing
as fat Baskin Cole & Bobby Baynard
rassled into
The Bluegrass Country Kings.

They was picking
"Your Cheating Heart"
when the trouble started.
Two tables was tussled over
& the Schlitz light got knocked all
crazy so what I seen was a flicker
of faces & Carol Lee punching
on Baskin's back
& him screaming at Bobby,
"Have you ever been dead?
Have you ever been dead?"
& then Baskin he come down on
that Baynard boy with an atomic drop
that would make Gorgeous George
snort.
& that was that.

Lacy Brockmoor & Shorty pried
them apart & somehow Bobby
got back his breath
& The Bluegrass Country Kings
sang "Jambalaya"
& you'd a thought folks had forgot

Stephen E. Smith

what happened cept for how they was
looking sneaky sidewise & the way
they was whispering over their beer.

Course every face come up sudden
when Carol Lee & Bobby was leaving.
He just grinned back over his shoulder
& give her ass the sweetest little
squeeze & I swear he winked at Baskin.
Them Baynards can act right ugly
when they take a mind to.

Now I don't know nothing about who's
right & who's wrong.
I mean what other folks do ain't
none of my nevermind.
But I can tell you this: poor ole Baskin
knows the truth: ain't nobody in this whole
damn world feels sorry for fat.

Leroy Pinrawes Tells How in Detroit
a Porno Movie Was Something Like Love

I watched chevy ass-ends rattle
down the line till I seen them
in my sleep
course this was before things got so bad
back when everybody knew
it was going to get better

then one night a bunch of them detroit
five-and-dimers bought me a beer
& took me to see this porno
picture show, said, "leroy boy, now
that's what real love is like"
& them fellas was so serious about all
that coupling
you'd a thought they was watching
their mamas or something

so a few days later I'm working the line
& it just come to me—
a woman or a chevy's ass-end
don't make no damn difference
what keeps us humping
is that lie we tell ourselves
about it being better the next time

that night I packed my bags
& come on home to the farm
I figured if you're going to live
in detroit
you best always be in love

Stephen E. Smith

God's Wildest Hair

She was senile and pretty eat up
with the cancer so each morning
we put Aunt Martha behind the wheel
of an old Packard and let her drive
around in the field behind the house
so we didn't have to listen to her say
stuff like: "Birds are flying out of
that horse's ass" or "How'd these
tobacco worms get in my underpants?"
She liked to play the country music
on the car radio and never caused
any trouble till one day she got God's
wildest hair and figured she'd drive
to Tabor City. Luckily she decided
to write to her sister first
so she drove to Bullard's Office Supply,
right through the plate glass window,
got out and browsed, got back in
and drove off. We'll never know
for sure about the next part,
probably she hit between six to sixteen
cars as she floored it through town
and five more police cruisers wrecked
before they pulled her over going
seventy miles an hour down Midland Road
the wrong way in a '47 Packard
with bad kingpins. State Troopers
didn't think it was the least bit funny.
They charged her with DWI, resisting
arrest, leaving the scene of an accident
and about twenty other things
and when we laughed, they didn't,

but they let us take her home on
fifty dollars bail. About a month
later two deputies knocked on the door
and said they had a warrant for
Aunt Martha's arrest on account
of her failing to appear and we
said fine but you'll have to go to
the hospital, that's where she is,
dying with the cancer, and they said
not to worry, they'd speak to the judge,
but I don't think they did
because a month later two different
officers came to arrest her
and we said fine again but you'll
have to dig her up, we buried her
a week ago. They didn't even smile
but only said to send Aunt Martha's
driver's license and a copy of
the death certificate to the Clerk of
Court, so I drank a six pack and got her
license out of an old black pocketbook
she'd hid under her mattress along with
pictures of all her dead kin and I put
the whole mess in an envelope and wrote
in big letters on the death certificate
LICENSE PERMANENTLY REVOKED BY GOD
and mailed it.

Stephen E. Smith

A Carolina Man Recalls
a Girl Named Belinda

Five beers at Shorty's Tavern
took him back thirty years
to a Sampson County road
after a July thunder shower,
steam drifting from the wet asphalt,
and the girl in the yellow print dress
damp against his shoulder,
his Buick Roadmaster smooth
through the Carolina heat
all the way to Clinton
and a neon vacancy
at the Oak Grove Motor Court
where that girl stepped
from her print dress
and straddled him.
Five beers and she came
back like an old sorrow.
He tried to recall her name
but someone kept dropping quarters
into the jukebox and Shorty
wanted to talk about how
the South had changed.

The Horsefly Trick

to know best
how it works
catch yourself
a horsefly
not a bluebelly
nor a green
bloodsucker
but a regular
assbiting
horsefly
and bigfinger
some grease from
the balljoint
on your daddy's
john deere
and rub it
on his head
(the horsefly's
I mean)
and watch him
bolt straight
into the
sun

Stephen E. Smith

Taint

I

Red McNeill: I bought Willa Stipe
eight bottles of beer and a barbecue
dinner down at the Pig 'n Chicken,
but when I finally got her out into my
pickup all she give me was a little
taint.
Me: Taint? What's taint?
Red: Taint what I had in mind, that's
for sure.

II

Baskin Cole: Taint? Well, if you slaughter
hogs without a first frost the salted side
meat will go taint even in the cool of the
springhouse.
Me: The meat would be tainted?
Baskin: It'll poison a damn dog to death.

III

Leroy Pinrawes: I recall one time Pa come
limping home from that whorehouse at
Sugar Hill. He had the taint and Mama
wouldn't have nothing to do with him for
the longest while. Once you got it, taint
nothing you can do about it.
Me: It's that bad, huh?
Leroy: Worse even than that.

IV

Bushnell Hamp: Here's the best I can
figure it: if you was a big fat bluebelly
fly eating on a cow pie and some ole boy

come along and plucked out your wings and
dropped you in the chicken pen, the whole
damn world would be nothing but taint.
Me: Good Lord! That's taint?
Bushnell: Yep.

Stephen E. Smith

Rasslin the Hot

the heat was so mean
last summer
I heard tell it slaughtered
hogs & cured them in the sty

by mid-june fat baskin cole
had took to lowering hisself
down the well
up to his udders in still water
keep from frying in his own lard

ladies in thanie mcneill's
sewing circle spent july stewing
in the pews at the peachbottom
baptist church
I ain't never seen a woman yet
didn't believe suffering done
her soul some good

third monday in august
old man stackhouse got a gnat
up his nose on bentown road
& stroked out
he just laid in the dust till
the sun eat out his eyes

bushnell hamp said it weren't
no use bitching
said he'd been rasslin the hot
all his life & never got
nothing to show for it
cept a chapped ass

Leroy Pinrawes Describes
the H-Bomb Test at Eniwetok

Took a bunch of us enlisted boys
& hunkered us behind some sandbags
in the middle of the blackest ocean
in the middle of the darkest night
& said, "Put on these glasses & watch
this" & I could hear them counting:
three, two, one—

It's like coming home from the fields
after priming tobacco all day & the
house is pitch-black & your pa strikes
a safety match & touches it to the lamp
wick & it's just a tiny flicker there
in all that darkness & then he slides
the glass chimney down & the light
rolls out all around you, sudden &
pure & everywhere at once.

Stephen E. Smith

Capital Punishment: Shorty's Recipe

take all them death row prisoners
& herd them into one big stadium
get the two best football teams ever
the colts with johnny unitas
the giants with y a tittle
bring in some topless cheerleaders
& give them death row prisoners
all the hot dogs they can eat
all the beer they can drink &
play the best football ever was
& when there's one second left
& the score is all tied up
have unitas drop into the end zone
& lob a bomb to raymond berry
who catches it to win the game &
when them prisoners jump up to cheer
electrocute them

ain't nobody could claim it was
cruel & unusual punishment

Boone Cola Empty

"Got me a buffalo nickel
for a Boone Cola,"
Bushnell Hamp used to say
before he'd crank a cold one
from the cooler
down at the Flying-A Station.

Daniel Boone & his dog
was painted white on the
bottle just over the lie
"A Boon to Health"
which Leroy Pinrawes claimed
was true words.

"Drink a Boone Cola before bed,
wake up with a blue steel,"
he used to say
& Bushnell sweared it made
snuff dribble tasty as
marzipan.

I recall Daughtry McLamb
stuck a shook bottle up
under Linda Kay Pusey's
crinolines & let go.
He said later she squealed that
same squeal once in the
back seat of his Kaiser.

Ain't made Boone Cola in years
but the bottles
is still around

Stephen E. Smith

kind of faded & grimy
in the kudzu out behind
what was the Flying-A Station.

Stumbled on one the other day
& just stood there thinking
how Leroy he sells mobile homes
in Taylortown now & how
Linda Kay she's secretary
to some lawyer in Maxton.
Hell, Daughtry McLamb's been dead
I guess twenty years.

But when I showed that empty
to Bushnell he said it weren't
worth nothing no more cause
there ain't a thimble full of
true Boone Cola left in the
whole world.
He said, "Red, you might just
as well toss that old bottle
in the dump. Ain't nobody with
any sense would give you a
buffalo nickel for an empty
Boone Cola."

Riding It Down

One summer I worked construction
on high-rises way up in the Texas sky
and one of them Mexican boys who was
about sixteen-years-old named Poncho
lifted up a sheet of 4 x 8 plywood and
just happened to catch hisself a breeze
off Galveston Bay. I watched him dance
backwards till he was maybe an inch
from falling twelve stories straight down.
Then that wind slackened off a bit
and he let out this loud yip yip
and held that sheet of plywood
even higher up in the sky.

They was always doing that, Mexicans,
laughing at the wind, tormenting white
cops down those dark Houston streets,
just daring everything. But this time
another harder wind hit the
building and lifted ole Poncho off
his feet and took him over the edge
quick as you can snap your fingers.
I could see his eyes just before
he went and it's a look you don't never
want to see. Like when it comes
clear all of a sudden that the joke's
on you. And for keeps.

Ole Poncho did what I'd do: he took
his only chance and rode the plywood down.
It was a slow fall, lazier than you might
think, the board sliding back and forth,

Stephen E. Smith

poor Poncho spread-eagle, floating away,
getting smaller all the time, until he
was just a speck, then a little poof
of dust rising from the foundation.

For years I thought on what it was might
have gone through Poncho's head them last
few seconds and I figure it was like when Pa
got the cancer. First off he was pissed,
then surprised, and when the truth settled
in he got damn desperate and finally he
just give up and rode it on down.

That night after they'd dragged Poncho's body
off to the Houston morgue, his buddies sat
talking round a fire burning in an oil drum.
They were growed men who talked in Mex,
but I asked one fellow who spoke some English
what it was they were saying. He handed me
a bottle of wine in a paper bag and laughed.
"You can't trust the wind," was all he told me.

note

just wanted you to know
that I drank
the Blue Ribbon
that was in
the refrigerator

because
there wasn't nothing
else in there
for breakfast

I ain't sorry
you weren't here
and I was so thirsty
and so glad

Bush

Stephen E. Smith

xxvi

so much depends
upon

a glass of
beer

glazed with
foam

beside the pickled
eggs

xxvii

Bush is
the coot
with cat
on his hat

After Five Bottles of Beer on the Front Porch Bushnell Has About Decided That It's All God's Fault

God and me sip beer
on the front porch while
pretty women
pass by in the street.

God says, "So you've
about decided that
it's all my fault
you can't have every
woman you want."

Suddenly I know
that God hears what
I'm thinking,
so I reach into the
cooler for that last
cold brew.

But God's hand
is there first.
He snaps off the bottle
cap with his teeth,
drains the bottle dry
and belches thunder.

I try not to think
what I'm thinking.
God laughs like hell.
"Listen," he says,
"you're right:
ain't nobody nowhere
ruder than me."

Stephen E. Smith

Stopping by the Bar on
a Summer Evening

Whose beer this is I think I know.
He is in the men's room, though;
He will not see me stopping here
To drain his mug filled up with beer.

His girlfriend must think him queer
To be left alone while I am near
Us two strangers on the make
the hottest night of the year.

She gives her earrings a little shake
To ask if there is some mistake.
The only other sound's the slur
Of Willie on the Wurlitzer.

This woman is flashy, dark and cheap,
But she has no promises to keep,
And miles to go before she sleeps,
And miles to go before she sleeps.

Bushnell Hamp Tells How
He Took Up with Dixie Fennel

All night I guzzled Schlitz and
listened to the lies on the jukebox.
All night I tapped my fingers
on the Formica and wondered
if there's one thing in this life
that's purely true.

And damn if it wasn't right there
Thumb tacked above the cash register,
this picture of a sailor kissing
a nurse the day the war ended.
I seen how that nurse lifted
one foot from the asphalt,
how both her arms hung limp
and how that sailor just crumpled
her up like you would the cellophane
off a pack of Luckys.

I knew that kiss was purely true
but nothing else come to mind
till I stopped short at the men's
room door to watch Dixie Fennell
squeak chalk on a pool cue.

I seen how she stretched her body
against the mahogany rail,
how she held one leg
straight for balance
and how in the smoky light her
tits just brushed the green felt—
then the slap of the eight ball
home in the corner pocket.

Stephen E. Smith

I snapped a quarter
down on that pool table,
lit me up a Lucky and said,
"Dixie, honey, rack 'em up."

Lindsey Lou Hamp Tells How
to Take the Head Off a Rooster

See how this old cock's neck
goes stiff on the stump?
I'll just leave him calm down
so when I do take his head off
I can watch him run crazy
like Bushnell done that time
he took up with Dixie Fennell.

Ever tell you about that?

Right after Bush run off
I got word him and Dixie
was keeping house in a trailer
this side of Tabor City
so I drove down and knocked
on their front door.
When it opened
there stood Bushnell Hamp nekkid,
a beer can in his hand
and his ole pecker stiffer
than this rooster's neck.

I said, "Bushnell Hamp you're
a growed man with obligations."
And he said, "Lindsey Lou I ain't
obligoddamngated to nogoddamnbody!"
And he slammed that trailer door,
which made a sound about like I felt.

Course I knowed he'd come home,
once his mind got right.

Stephen E. Smith

You see, Bush is like this old rooster,
sometimes his body gets a whole lot
stronger than his head.

Well now look here,
this old bird's gone slack on me,
so I'll just ease his neck
onto this stump and think about
how I don't blame Bushnell
for nothing that happened.

Hand me that ax.
Watch this.

The Goddamn-A-Thon

for Richard Hood

Goddamn if that goddamn
woman didn't knock at the
goddamn door and I'm
drinking a goddamn beer
and goddamnit I gotta
get off the goddamn couch
and go open the goddamn door
and there's this goddamn woman
with the goddamnest look
on her goddamn face and god
damn if she didn't goddamn
say:
Goddamnit Bush,
you got goddamn obligations
and goddamnit your goddamn
ass better get goddamn home
pretty goddamn soon.
That's what she goddamn
said,
goddamnit.

Stephen E. Smith

Gettin Even

anyhow it was bushnell hamp who
told us that being married wasn't as
romantic as hemorrhoids & so some
of us boys went down to rockfish
where his crippled wife kept him
penned up like the hound he is & we
heaved dirt clods & hollered till we
shamed him off on a three week drunk

course we couldn't know that by
way of gettin even that little woman
would get herself spaded
had all her tubes tied up or some
thing so there'd be no little
bushnells to drink hooch & whore
who the hell's to say what gets
into women these days

now bushnell he mostly mopes & says
there won't be nobody left to piss on
his grave & saturday nights we
hunker against shag's chevy pickup
guzzling schlitz & singing c&w to
some jackleg station outta Clinton

I mean there just ain't much we can say
that little split-tail might have
a crippled up hip but she can sure
as hell kick ass better than most

Bushnell Hamp Tells What Went Wrong with America Somewhere South of Coats Crossroads

"Eisenhower," says Bushnell Hamp.
"You could drive a ten-penny nail
between that man's eyes and he'd
go right on grinning."

At Newton Grove we turn north.
Beer cans rattle like rats down
the floorboard. Bush's pickup
slaps the tracks and we shimmy
off the shoulder on highway 701.
"Bad kingpins," he says. "Front
end of this Dodge loose as that
tight widow I've been wanting to
pork."

At Clayton we crack a cold six
and Bush says, "I do believe that
Willow Springs widow might be
worth smoking over. That thing's
probably rusted shut, but she might
be up for a little action."

Just south of Coats Cross Roads
Bush unracks his .22 and we climb
out to take a leak. "Truth is,"
he says, "that widow, this pickup
and America all got the same damn
problem."

Stephen E. Smith

Bushnell Hamp takes aim.
Bushnell Hamp pumps 18 slugs into
the door of his Dodge pickup.
"Yes sir," he says, "just ain't
no denying the fact we all got a
little too much mileage on us."

How It Is

Like just last night I cut back by
Bracey's Corner where Daughtry McLamb's
widow gets by best she can on GI
insurance & there was this regular
whirligig of yard apes kicking up
dust front of her trailer & so I
pulled over to see if maybe it was
a girl fight or something & you know
that woman had chained her boy who's
about eight or so to a chinaberry
tree & dressed him up in a little
girl's dress cause of something he'd
done bad & left him there for folks
to rag at & all them kids was hooting
& heaving beer cans & gravel & that
boy was screaming & straining at his
chains like a hound with the hydro
phobia.

Now I'll tell you, it's damn hard not
to see yourself as every kid that
hurts & I had half a mind to run them
brats off but then I recalled my pa
saying once, "Bushnell, you wouldn't be
the man you are today if I hadn't
kicked your young ass once in a while"
& it occurred to me that maybe that's
just how it is & so I popped the
clutch & burned rubber till I couldn't
think no more & now what's bothering me
is nothing does.

Stephen E. Smith

Linkage

"Like a baby asleep in the bullrushes,"
Preacher Monroe said at the funeral,
was how they found JT Baynard after his
'54 Merk jumped the blacktop
coming round that curve near Newcomb.
Course all of us down here at Shorty's
knew it was bad linkage,
JT missing a gear, probably downshifting,
him depending on things in this world
going just so.

So twenty years later
when they found JT's baby brother Bobby
dead on the same curve, us boys
looked at each other and knew
what the hell had happened: a few beers
and Bobby dwelling on his big brother JT,
trying to figure—
like all us boys here
at Shorty's is trying to figure—
just what the hell it is
always goes wrong.

Saturday, August 19, 2000

I ate me some brains and eggs for breakfast and about ten I drove over to Baskin's to help him change out the water pump on that '51 Ford convertible he's been working on for 40 years. One of the bolt holes was stripped so we drove my truck down to NAPA and bought us a heli-coil repair kit, rethreaded the hole, and torqued on the new pump. Then we buffed up the 17-inch Signature wheels with them new Nitto NT radials, polished the 2½-inch stainless headers, detailed the 350 V-8, and washed the clear-coated solar yellow urethane paint.

We drove to Shorty's for lunch. I drank three Bud Lights and ate a Penrose Tijuana Mama hot sausage and a pickled egg. Baskin didn't eat nothing. I'll bet he's lost 100 pounds since he started chemo. We watched the NASCAR race at the Michigan Speedway on TV and then rode around with the top down. At the light on Glebe and Glenwood some kids pulled up with that rap shit pounding out of big bass speakers. "What is it about those pissants that makes them believe I want to hear their music?" Baskin asked.

I went home and tried to fix the front door hinge and swore I'd never buy another Oakwood Home. The air conditioner is busted and it must have been 130 inside that aluminum coffin. I opened the windows and turned on the fan but it didn't do no good.

Stephen E. Smith

I microwaved a Lean Cuisine Cheese Cannelloni and drank three more Bud Lights. I should've taken a shower but the bathtub drain was clogged so I pulled on a clean tee-shirt and jeans.

About eight I stopped by Lindsey Lou's. She don't go out much since her mama died but her air conditioner works good. We watched *East of Eden* on AMC and she said we'd seen the movie at the drive-in back when we were dating so I said to change the channel to wrestling. She said, "You know what the trouble with you is? You want to do just wherever it is you want to do." I said okay we didn't have to watch wrestling but could she get me a beer and damn if she didn't get pissy. "If you want a beer go buy it your own damn self. I ain't fetching beer for my ex-husband." I got up and walked out the door. "Bushnell Hamp," I could hear her yelling after me, "you always was an asshole."

Riding with Bedford Forrest

Fishing in Peachbottom Creek
I caught me a snapping turtle,
a ten-pounder who tugged my
bamboo pole almost double.

I was maybe ten years old
and I wanted back my line,
hook, sinker, and bait.
But that snapper had swallowed
all of it and judging from
his attitude, meant to keep it.

So I dragged him down the bank,
head wagging like a dog's tail,
and asked my great-grandpappy
who was 102 and had rode with
Bedford Forrest during the war
if he could get the hook out.
He was napping under a crack willow

but he unfolded like a jackknife till
he stood straight up taller than
you'd believe and snatched a hatchet
from his tackle box and cut that
turtle's head clean off
so sudden that I staggered flat
back against the bank.

He stomped one brogan down
on that turtle's head,
jammed a stick between the jaws
and with this terrible tearing

Stephen E. Smith

noise yanked my hook, line,
sinker and bait out of that
turtle's mouth, and kicked his
head into the water, where it
sank, still snapping, into the
mud. Then he folded up against
the willow and fell sound asleep.

"Thanks," I said.

Kilpatrick's Shirt-Tail Skedaddle

Riding into a sleeping camp, the Confederate Cavalrymen
were able to put the entire Federal command, including
the General himself, to flight in less than a minute. . . .
To make his escape "Little Kil" had to spring from
the warm bed of his lovely lady.

—J. G. Barrett,
The Civil War in North Carolina

The whole command was flying before the most
formidable cavalry charge I have ever witnessed.

March 11, 1865
J. Kilpatrick, Brevet Major-General
Official Record

"Bushnell," he'd say. "Bush, how about
fetching me a quart of that clear stumphole
hooch your clever daddy done hid out near the
springhouse." Once I'd done that,
he'd tote it down to Puppy Creek & cut
it just so with white rock water. Always
he'd add one ripe peach sliced & a tablespoon
of sweet clover honey. The crock he'd
leave covered with a damp cloth maybe a
week & then every day the old man would
take a shot warm in one swallow. He'd say
"Bush, have a sip for your own self.
If it don't kill you outright could be
you'll live a hundred years like your
great-grandpappy here."

I can't claim for certain it was the
tangle-leg kept him kicking but the fact
remains that old bag of bones buried three
wives & twelve children & then dragged his
moth-balled biscuit box from Scuffletown
to Rockfish where he spent his last three

Stephen E. Smith

years telling me them stories it had took
him the other hundred to get just right.

I was maybe ten when he came to live with us,
but I can recall he'd sing a song for every
story he told, like "Pretty Sparrow" for
his boy Butler killed in Cuba & "All the
Good Times Are Past & Gone" thinking of
his first wife Ozell who was took with the
typhoid & of course his favorite "Rebel
Soldier" about how he hated the Constitution
& the eagle with its squall & how he hated
the goddamn thieving Yankees worst of all.

Once he'd sung through six verses, you'd hear
about the war, hear about how on the Lickskillet
Road a good brass belt buckle stopped a
minie ball or else the time grapeshot ripped
his ear near Snapfinger Creek ("Bush, another
inch & you wouldn't been born. Think on
that, why don't you?") & if you were lucky
he'd tell how he'd rode with General Joe
Wheeler & how once they'd caught the Yankee
scoundrel Judson Kilpatrick hard at it & run
him from a pretty woman's bed bare-ass naked
into the cold dawn.

He'd cock his whiskey-burned face up
close to mine & whisper, "Bush, you wanta
hear what it were like when the world went
crazy?" Of course it didn't make no difference
what you wanted, you were going to hear
about it anyhow & so that old man would rear

back sudden & squeal, "Lord God, that son
of a bitch Sherman laid us open like a gutted
sow, from Savannah to Cheraw weren't nothing
left standing in the pine stubble cept scorched
chimneys & tombstones & us boys riding with
Wheeler always just a short trot ahead, living
off hog fat, pone dodgers, & sometimes
some sassafras tea."

He knew now he had you, so he'd ease off
& sigh, "Bush," he'd say then, "we done
rode so far that last spring the bottom was
wore right outta my butternut britches & I
was stitching a patch in a mulberry orchard
down near the Devil's Gut, my mind studying
as usual on hot biscuits & molasses, when
Captain Bostic allowed we was going to have
us a tussle. Seems one of Shannon's scouts
had spied Kilpatrick & his troopers holed
up at some country cross roads, said that
Yankee scoundrel had a Columbia belle, one
Miss Mary Boozer, his captive in the Monroe
house & that he was scheming a saber attack
on the soft underbelly of Southern womanhood.

"We was right away in the saddle, all two
thousand of us, cause we wanted General
Judson Kilpatrick, a bluebelly vermin who
done burned his way cross three states,
doing all the mischief he might & it was
told around he'd stole every silver
service in South Carolina. So we rode
most that night & drawed up near dawn

in the pine dark around the Yankee camp.
Word was 'no talking' but this Texas
green stick beside me kept going on about
how one time he'd seen this Mary Boozer,
about how she was as fine a piece of female
flesh as you'd likely lay eyes on, how
the seams of her bodice was stretched
tighter than feed sacks & her hair was
yellower than wild susans. Hell, my vitals
was growing right firm when the Captain
yelled 'All right boys, let's put it to 'em!'
I dug in my spurs sudden & that old
clay-bank sorrel I was riding gave a snort.

"Bush, there ain't never been a bunch
of fellas surprised like them bluebellies
was when we went whipping through the
blackjack & turkey oak right in on top
of them—boots & blankets, mules & muskets
gone all which ways, us graybacks giving
them the old yip-yip & the Yankees scrambling
in their scanties, hell it was like falling
through the roof of a hen house: everywhere
confusion—horses screaming, Captain Bostic
yelling orders there weren't no hearing
for the racket, some fool puffing a bugle.
I seen a belly-shot trooper double over
in the saddle & that big-talking Texas
boy went down sprawling, & it occurred
to me maybe I oughta ease on over beside
the Monroe house where there was less of a
rumpus.

"It was there I seen what I seen. I'd
just swiveled the ramrod on my Enfield when
this little hawk-faced fella come climbing
outta the window wearing nothing but a shirt,
that dead fuse dangling twixt his bandy
legs, & you'd a thought he was some kind of
peculiar the way he wagged right up to
Captain Bostic & chatted, maybe saying
how-ja-do while the minie balls was whistling
all around. Course that little fella was
Kilpatrick hisself & he just pointed into
the woods & that bamboozled Bostic went
galloping off (I ain't never knowed an
officer yet could tell a mule's ear from
a Memphis strumpet) & then that Kilpatrick
yanked one of his own blueboys off a horse,
jumped on with a yelp! & skedaddled, balls
& bare ass bouncing into the dawn.

"He got hisself clean away, & Bush, since
I seen it for my own self, I ain't never let
no preacher tell me there's justice in this
life & as for Bostic, well, we forgive him.
Truth is it's damn hard to tell a private's
privates from a general's, & there just ain't
no judging the meat by the size of the sausage."
Then that old man would lean back & cough
up a dry cackle, all that was left of his
laugh. It was a joke he always enjoyed
right well. But when he'd wiped the tears
from his eyes, he'd get serious & say,
"Course that ain't nothing to what I seen next.
& what I seen was a woman. That dead

Stephen E. Smith

Texas boy had spoke true. I ain't laid
eyes on nothing compared to her fore or
since. She had a face more perfect than
any & so beautiful I can't make you imagine.
Took my breath, her standing there so
sudden in the doorway, wearing a flimsy
thin nightdress, all that yellow hair
tumbling down round her white shoulders
& her eyes (even in the smokelight I
could see they was so clear blue) wide with
puzzlement. She had one hand on the
doorframe, the other lifting the hem of
her nightdress nicely over her knees. She
stood there straight as a poplar, graceful
as a willow, & when she seen me she took
three sweet steps forward, her udders
rustling to & fro neath soft cotton, &
said, 'Sir, I have been deceived by a
Yankee villain & I implore you to act
in my behalf & in such a manner as to
redeem my honor."

"Bush, if ever a man was struck stupid
it was your great-grandpappy as he stared
at that handsome woman. Hell,
I didn't have sense enough to even answer
but only said out loud, 'Benjamin Gorham
Hamp, whatever befalls you after now ain't
going to signify for nothing.' Just no
knowing how long I stared—sometimes it
seems like forever—but I can tell you this:
it was a trifle too long. Some Yankee
drawed a bead on me with a Spencer & what

come next was like a white-hot slap in
the face. Sweet Mary Boozer was the last
I seen of life till everything was done.
Not the battle, the war. It was most of a
month or more later before my head healed
good enough for me to come awake at Ozell's
place down near Bones Creek.

"My eyes opened there in the late-April dark.
Beyond the cabin window I could hear the
bullfrogs humping & chuck-will's-widow
whistling him home. I reckon I'd been
wrong-headed all them days, cause I could
see her still, that beautiful woman,
white-gowned & big-bosomed, bright as a
bay blossom you'd shudder to touch.

"Ozell's husband had fell at Sharpsburg
& when I was well we married & I made her
a breadboard so I'd have hot biscuits
& molasses with every meal. But Bush, after
all this time, after all them wives &
babies I buried, after all the cold winters
& ruined crops I seen, when my mind comes
again to studying on that Mary Boozer,
standing there before me like everything
a man could ask of this life, always just
a fingertip away, why, it's some kind of
old hunger comes over me for sure."

Then he'd smile & point at his crotch.
"Why looky there," he'd cackle. "I do
believe that old soldier is standing
at attention."

Stephen E. Smith

The day they buried FDR the old man took
down with a fever. I asked him if he was
going to do like the president done & die.
"Die!" he said. "Why that sounds right
tedious. I ain't never going to die—though
for a fact I about did once." & he told
me of one time when he'd had a growth in
his throat & about how the doctor said it
would kill him by smothering his breath.
"Well Bush," he said, "when that growth
got too bothersome I just reached my fingers
down my mouth like this & pulled it out.
It's round this house still, in a pickle
jar full of alcohol. I saved it to remind
me what a man might have to do to keep
hisself alive."

But that night he couldn't hold the
tangle-leg on his stomach & the next
morning he was just dead. Nobody knew
where Ozell rested, so we buried him at
Longstreet, next to his second wife Sarah.
Weren't much left to say at the grave.
I mean, even if there ain't no heaven,
you couldn't rightly say he'd been swindled.
After the funeral I asked my pa about
that pickle jar full of alcohol. He just
laughed. "Boy," he said, "you ought to
know by now there weren't nothing ever
come outta that old man's face you could
take for truth."

Benjamin Gorham Hamp
Tells How

in dead january
the memory sheds flesh
& faces fade like calico

you go from the graveyard
deep into the pine wood

& sit so quiet
the wind could be voices
you know ain't there

make a fire against the cold
& just listen
Listen

Stephen E. Smith